TRAINING HORSES

Janine Verschure

TRAINING HORSES

REBO PUBLISHERS

© 2003 Zuid Boekprodukties
© 2006 Rebo Publishers

Text and photographs: Janine Verschure
Cover design and layout: Minkowsky Graphics, Enkhuizen, The Netherlands
Typesetting and pre-press services: A.R. Garamond, Prague, The Czech Republic
Proofreading: Sarah Dunham, Jeffrey Rubinoff

ISBN 13: 978-90-366-1116-9
ISBN 10: 90-366-1116-4

CONTENTS

FOREWORD

Good training is the beginning and also the basis of good cooperation with your horse. You can only get good cooperation from a well-trained horse. A well-trained horse is an undamaged horse that has not lost its trust in human beings during its training, but is sufficiently experienced that it has nothing to fear. You can only convince a horse of your good intentions by approaching it in the correct manner.

We will assume that the horse that will be trained is one that has never been ridden before. A green horse would therefore be a horse that does not have any experience as a riding horse. An inexperienced animal that has had little to no negative experience from human contact will not behave aggressively that easily.

Problem horses that display aggressive behavior are too complicated and dangerous to discuss here, although biting, bucking and not walking with the halter will be discussed. This sort of behavior is displayed by every young horse, and as a rule can be stopped with proper training. A horse that literally tries to attack or hit (kick with its hind leg) is not unknown; this aggressive behavior mostly stems from negative experiences. It is wise to try and determine the cause of the aggressive behavior before trying to resolve it. Needless to say, aggressive behavior can be very dangerous. If you own such a difficult animal, do not try and train it yourself but leave it in the hands of an experienced trainer. Explain the exact nature of the horse's problem so that the trainer will know where to start.

Janine Verschure

1. PRIOR
CONSIDERATIONS

Purpose of training

Trust is the keyword during the training process. The most important part of training consists of building trust between the animal and humans. You will see the word trust very often; this underscores its importance. Ensure that you gain and keep the trust of the horse; without trust you will only be able to impose your will on the horse, but not train it. We will assume that the final goal of the training of the horse is riding it in dressage – with a saddle. Dressage is the basis of competitive riding. You can also tackle other disciplines in competitive riding with an obedient horse, but it always begins with dressage.

Experience

An inexperienced rider cannot train a horse. However, it is impossible to give a guideline of the level of experience a rider must have in order to be able to train a horse. Some beginner competitive riders compete on the lowest level of basic riding, but work so well with horses that they can tame a horse sufficiently to accept a saddle on its back through sheer ability, without any problems. However, it is possible that problems could occur with further training, when it must be made clear to the horse what the saddle is

*Left: Dressage is
the basis of
competitive sport*

*Right: Assistance
is indispensable*

*Experience is very
important*

meant for and how it should react to it. The stage where the
work must be fine-tuned is when the horse is being prepared to be competition ready. A rider with limited experience will not have the ability to speak in clear language to the
horse. On the other hand, many experienced competitive
riders have so little feeling for riding that they would never
be able to train a horse. We will cautiously assume that a
rider in the easy to medium-difficult class of the basic dressage sport, who has achieved a reasonable score, will be able
to train a horse.

Risks

Even riding a well-trained and reliable horse can be dangerous. As with other sports, horseback riding is not without risks. Training a young horse can be especially risky. In the first place, training a horse can be a risk to your own health. The result of bad training can also create risks; a scared, ill-mannered or even aggressive horse is dangerous to its rider. Few horses come into this world already spoiled. An important part of the horse's character is formed by people. If you cannot ensure that your horse will come through the most important phase of its life – the training phase – undamaged, leave the training to someone else.

Help

You cannot train a horse without help. You will need help during longeing, and it is unwise to ride an inexperienced horse without anyone else standing around. It is always necessary to be careful when you are handling a young horse, so it is best to ask an experienced fellow horse enthusiast to assist.

It is also better to have someone else in the vicinity even when the animal is saddle-tame, or see to it that someone frequently comes to have a look if you are still sitting in the saddle. Finally: even when your animal is obedient and you trust it sufficiently to carry on alone with the training, always carry a cellular phone in your pocket. If the need arises it is always easy to phone for help.

2. HORSE BEHAVIOR

Leadership in the horse world

When the aim of training is to build a bond of trust with your horse, leadership is not the most appropriate word. Cooperation is not everything though; the horse must be shown who is boss from time to time.

In the wild, horses have structured societies. The highest placed mare is the leader of the herd in close cooperation with the most dominant stallion, also known as the alpha animal. The dominant mare is the day-to-day leader while the most important task of the dominant stallion (other than mating) is the protection of the herd. Young, strong

Horses educate each other

stallions are chased away because they can pose a challenge to the leadership of the dominant stallion.

Leadership: human to horse

The only way to educate your horse properly is for you to take the leading role. Needless to say, people that have a feeling for horses will do this naturally. They will take on the role of the leader (dominant mare) and protector (stallion) automatically. If you are able to do this then communication with the horse will be easy. Some horses realize automatically that humans are dominant but there are also horses that will try to overstep these boundaries, as a result of their sex (stallions often do this) or youthful enthusiasm. I want to emphasize that this is not universal and most horses will usually accept your leadership without question,

Leadership from human to horse

but sometimes you will need to dictate the boundaries very clearly.

Dominance

If you are not exuding natural dominant signals to the horse, you can learn how to do this by adjusting your attitude and behavior. If you come shuffling into the stable with downcast eyes, the horse will probably not even look up from its hay. If you enter at a firm pace with an upright head and allow the animal to sniff at your hand as a greeting, the animal will realize that the boss has arrived. An overly loud "good afternoon" is not appropriate though. Nor should you run into the stable; this will be seen as a threat.

Acceptance of new leadership

It is very important that you do not let yourself be pushed aside in your horse's living area. Firstly you must greet the horse and then walk freely through the stable or the pen. The horse must make space for the boss, not the other way around. If the horse tries to remove you from his territory, punish the behavior. Push the horse away and use your

voice. Mares also punish their foals in the horse world without any grudges being held. As soon as the animal has been
punished the matter should be seen as dealt with and over
and you should start with a clean slate. Mares and geldings
seldom question leadership. A stallion, by contrast, wants to
chase away competition through sheer instinct and may
want to dominate you.

Breaking in a stallion?

Anyone who loves horses will be charmed by the beauty of an adult stallion. They are naturally muscled and their shining hide makes any horse owner proud. But: a stallion is heavily influenced by its instincts, which are stronger than its willingness to obey its rider. In the hands of an experienced rider, a stallion can be a very obedient and good companion. However, with an inexperienced rider on its back, a stallion that is ready to mate can hold danger for its rider as well as its immediate environment. The owner of a stallion should be experienced to such a level that he/she should not have any questions about the training of a young horse; the breaking-in of stallions is not discussed in this book.

Haflinger stallion

Haflinger mare

*Literally chasing
the horse away
from the herd*

Red card

In the (semi) wild, foals are educated by their dam and, when it is necessary, the dominant stallion helps out somewhat. Animals that do not live within the rules of the herd are immediately punished. If this behavior does not subsequently improve, they are chased away from the herd. The transgressor is only allowed back when it shows obvious remorse. Our horses do not like being "chased away" or "pushed away" either. You can use this method to educate your horse during the course of daily contact. You can punish your horse by "sending it away" and subsequently reward it by allowing it back into the "herd."

*The boss is
accepted as the
leader: The horse
follows her
through the area*

Monty Roberts' "Joining up" method

The famous horse whisperer Monty Roberts has developed a method based on the principle of "joining up":
The horse is allowed to roam freely in a longeing circle and then physically chased away by its boss. No violence is used here. For instance, you can use a soft piece of rope to chase the horse away, and look at the horse with a serious expression on your face. The horse will react to this by "running away" in the longeing circle and galloping around its boss. After a while the animal will become tired from all the running and will want to "negotiate" about the dominant position of the boss. The horse does this by bending its head, making chewing movements and licking its lips. When this happens the boss should take on a less dominant attitude and should not look at the horse with such a serious expression. By then turning his upper body away, he invites the animal to come back to it. This can be explained as follows: a dominant horse that turns its body by 45 degrees in regards to another animal is exposing its weak side. By doing this, the dominant animal is indicating that the situation is over and the other horse may approach its herd member. When the horse approaches its boss it can be rewarded ("taking it back into the herd"). An experienced horse whisperer such as Roberts knows that if he can get the horse to follow him through the entire longeing circle the horse has accepted his leadership.

The best reward a horse can wish for: grazing in the pasture

Rewarding

Good training cannot be accomplished without rewards. An effective way of rewarding a horse is by gently scratching its mane. By doing this you imitate the way horses declare their friendship toward each other by nibbling on each other at the necks. Most horses like this very much. Some horses like it when you scratch them gently on the forehead or the top of the mane. There has never been a horse that enjoyed a hard smack on the neck or the loins. When you pat it gently on the neck and speak to it in a friendly tone of voice, it will quickly understand that you are rewarding it. Although opinions about this are divided, I am of the opinion that a reward in the form of a snack or some scraps cannot do any harm. The animal will understand immediately that this is the correct way and that you are happy with its behavior. Do not overdo this though. When you notice that the horse is begging it is wise to give it fewer snacks in the future. The best reward after some hard work is of course some rest. When a horse is doing its

Well done!

best and it indicates that it wants to cooperate, it will certainly appreciate being allowed back into its pen or stable.

Good boy

It is recommended that you say "good boy" to the horse in a friendly tone of voice. The horse will then associate the words "good boy" with a reward. As time goes by it will realize that it is being rewarded by you just saying "good boy."

It is not known if the horse recognizes the words themselves or the way the words are spoken as to whether it is being punished or rewarded. It is therefore best not to use words or phrases that could sound similar to the horse but have very different meanings, such as "good boy" and "bad boy."

Determining boundaries

Sometimes it may be necessary to tell a young horse how the relationship works: "Until here and no further; I am the boss." Unfortunately some people are of the opinion that a horse can be convinced by beating it. If you take this to be a correct method, the end result of your "training" will be a horse spoilt for life. Before you punish a horse, you must understand that the animal is not acting like that because it does not understand or because of fear, but because it is disputing your leadership. An animal that does not understand why it is being punished will lose its trust in its boss. It will do wonders if at the moment that the horse is being punished (by pulling it with a yank of the rope or a tap with a whip) you speak to the horse with an angry and low "bad!" The animal will in this way associate the words with being punished. When you have done this twice already only the spoken word "bad!" will be sufficient to punish the

I am the boss!

horse the third time. It speaks for itself that you should never whip a horse!

Self control

Self control is indispensable when dealing with horses. With force and anger, you will only be able to make a horse scared of you. It is possible that you will climb back on your horse very angrily after you have fallen off. You can use this anger to beat your fear of getting back on again after falling off but do not make the (human) mistake of taking your anger out on your horse. It will at some points feel as if the horse is bleeding you completely dry, but never punish an animal through sheer anger. By simply counting to ten many horse owners have been avoided a fit of anger that they would may have regretted later on. On top of this, punishment through anger normally has the opposite effect. A well known example is that of a horse in the pasture that does not want to be caught. There are few horse owners that would still be cheerful after following their horses for half an hour through the pasture. When your horse is walking away from you, take note of its body language. If it is behaving in a very dominant way, walk very upright, look at the animal with a serious expression – this means the horse is less likely to run away from you – and shout its name out very loudly. When the animal finally comes back, reward it, however difficult that may be. If such a horse is punished at that moment you can rest assured that it will run away again the next time. A way to prevent this is for your arrival to be associated with something nice: a bit of petting or a snack, for instance.

3. THE BEGINNING: FOALS

Foals

If your horse is in your possession since its birth you can immediately start training it, because early training consists mostly of creating a bond with the foal. A newly born animal is in the interpreting phase: any impressions it may get will be remembered later on. If you rub the foal dry directly after its birth it will get to know you very quickly. It will automatically accept you as a safe haven, along with

Still so much to learn

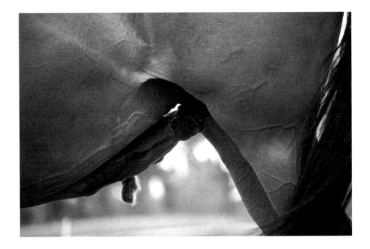

its dam. If the mare does not want your help or if the foal is really scared, do not press the issue. The foal must drink its dam's milk as quickly as possible after birth as it contains antibodies that are invaluable in the fight against infections. It is therefore essential that you allow the animals to calmly go their own way and not disturb their own bonding. During standard daily care the animal will learn to trust you. It is not necessary to spend hours on end there every day: ten to fifteen minutes per day is sufficient for a foal that still suckles to be aware of your presence.

Mother's instinct

The character of even the sweetest and most reliable mare can change when her mother's instinct comes to the fore. It is possible that the mare will become very protective of its foal. Be very careful when you are going to get in contact with its foal and put the mare at ease before you approach its foal. When it is reacting particularly aggressively to your presence, it is wise to leave it to be a mother before you request the attention of the foal. If the dam still cannot stand your interference after a few days you should seek help from an experienced horse trainer; if you cannot approach the foal it is losing out on a good education.

Getting used to human touch

When the foal is used to your presence you can begin to prepare it for its later years as a riding horse. Lift the hooves of the foal regularly. Start with the left front hoof and face the backside of the foal. Before you pick the hoof

up, touch the leg very carefully. Make sure that the animal does not get frightened by your touch. Soothe the animal until it relaxes and then touch the entire leg. You can only start picking up the hooves when the animal has accepted your touch. Do this while giving commands like "foot" or "lift foot." For the first time, it is sufficient to pick the hooves up and immediately put them down (gently!) again. You can let the time the animal has to stand on three legs build up later on and then also touch the bottom of the hooves. Next you have to pick the left hand back hoof up, then right hand front and finally the right hand back. It will put the foal at ease when it is familiar with the sequence and roughly knows what is happening. You will see that the animal will, as time goes on, pick the hooves up itself when you give it the command "lift foot." Touch the hooves of the foal frequently, as well as the ears. A foal that is used to this will be easier to train later on and will also give fewer problems when you are putting on the headset. When the foal is used to fingers in and around its mouth at a young age it will accept worm ino-culations and the bit more easily.

Left: Forge a friendship with the foal as soon as possible

Right: But allow it some rest as well

Weaning

A weaned foal is no longer being fed by its dam's milk. From the age of around three months, a foal develops more interest in the world around it. It will often go wandering through the grazing area and play more frequently and further from its dam. At around this period the milk production in the dam will be reduced and the first signs of the breaking of the tight bond between the mother and child will become visible. In the wild, a foal will only completely leave its dam after one year. We wean foals mostly when it is between four to six months old. If a foal is weaned after one year, chances are that it will grow up as a very immature "mamma's child." Most foals that are born during the springtime will spend only one summer with their dams. In ideal circumstances, this will be in the pasture with other horses and foals. The foals will learn very important social lessons from each other and from the adult horses.

Sensible weaning

Abruptly breaking the bond between the dam and its foal is not recommended. A foal that is suddenly taken away from its dam will be exposed to a great amount of stress. This can lead to a lot of energy being wasted, with it calling for its dam for hours on end. There is also the chance that it will lose its appetite and this will not be good for its development. Allow the process of weaning to come to a gradual end. For instance, you can put the dam and its foal in stables next to each other for a number of days so that the foal will not be able to drink from its dam anymore but will still have contact with it. Only once the foal is used to this situation can the mare be taken away. You can also take the foal away for short periods of time and let it eat in the stable. In this way the foal will have positive associations with the separation. The length of these separations should gradually be increased until the foal has considerably less stress about being weaned. After three to four weeks the mare and foal can graze together normally; the foal will not want to drink from its dam anymore.

Problem: dominance

The foal must also realize that you are the leader. You should therefore not tolerate any aggressive or dominant behavior. Use your voice to do this; an angry shout has just as much impact as a slap. Talk encouragingly to a foal when it is anxious, but raise your voice when it is testing

Does the grass taste delicious, Mom?

you. Straightforward aggression (biting, kicking) can be punished with a tap. It is better not to use your hands for this, because these same hands have to put the bridle on and comfort the animal. A push with the elbow or an angry shout often has the same effect.

Friendly approaches

Horses greet each other by sniffing each other and then blowing into each other's noses. They inhale each other's breath to recognize the other. The best way to make a friendly approach towards a horse is by letting it sniff your hand. It will recognize the smell of your hand. If the foal offers it you can blow softly into its nostril. After the first – often surprised – interested reaction, the foal will really appreciate this type of greeting. If a foal is looking for a brutal approach by pushing you aside, put it in its place by pushing it right back. Its dam will also do this.

Left: May I have a taste?

Right: Close to the dam it is safe

Biting stallions

Most stallions cannot resist it: the temptation to bite seems irresistible. A stallion cements his status by nibbling and softly biting a mare and there will inevitably be a moment when he will try this with you. During the summer, when you are not wearing much clothing, this would certainly not be appreciated. Many people proceed by hitting the horse on the nose, which is a very effective way for him to stop doing this. To be honest, it is understandable that you – from pure frustration about a blue mark on your forearm – will want to smack the animal. However, you run the risk that the animal will become "head shy" and afraid of your hands; such an animal will fall back when you want to pat him or put the bridle on.

Unfortunately many stallions are head shy. A better way to stop a stallion from biting is by grabbing him firmly by the halter and speaking to him in a friendly way while you pet his nose and head. Scratch the mane on his head and between his eyes, and make sure that he enjoys it when you do this. When the stallion tries to bite you, push his head – while you are holding the halter –away from you with force. The horse will feel as if he is being sent away from you. You should then pull his head back towards you and continue with the petting. This way he will learn that you do not want him close to you when he bites you, and he will be rewarded when he does not bite. To reinforce this you can even give the horse a snack, but within limits.

Horses look for friendship in this way

Approaching from the left

A horse should always be approached from the left hand side. When you are leading the horse with the halter, you should also walk on its left hand side. You must hold the halter rope in your right hand, close to its head, well under the hooks. The halter rope should run right in front of your body and with your left hand you should hold it tight – a good distance from your body. If the foal should pull loose from your right hand, you will still be holding it with your left hand. This means that the horse will be walking on your right with its shoulder next to yours.

Making a foal halter tame

It is sensible to make a foal halter tame as quickly as possible. This does not only mean that the animal can wear the halter, but also that you can put the halter on and take it off without any problems. Keep in mind that a scared animal never has any bad intentions. Stroke its entire head gently. If the foal stays calm while doing this you can put the halter on. As soon as the foal has accepted the halter, you can lead it with the halter. Start slowly at first and do not go too far from the mother. You will notice that the foal will protest when you lead it too far from its peers. Do not worry too much about this: the foal will have to learn that sometimes it has to suppress its herding instinct and be obedient.

The foal is not walking with you

If a scared foal does not want to walk with you, do not try and pull it with you with excessive force. Try to persuade it by talking to it and putting it at ease. If this is not working it is sensible to call for some assistance. Ask your assistant to push the foal gently forward or to tap it gently on the side. The person who is pushing the horse should not stand directly behind the foal: sharp foal hooves can seriously injure your assistant.

Whatever happens, do not give up! By giving up, the animal will learn that by refusing it will get its way. If a stubborn foal walks only one step with you, immediately let the halter relax, reward it elaborately and allow it to go back to the grazing field; there is no better reward for foals (yet).

Biting stallions

Make a foal used
to a halter as
quickly as
possible

The foal is bucking

When the foal is trying to pull back from the halter by
bucking (and it will try this at least once but most probably more often) there is only one good way to stop it from
doing this: by teaching the foal that resisting makes no
sense. Teach it that there is only one way to escape the
pressure of the halter, and that is to walk along willingly.
If a foal is trying to pull itself away from the pressure that
the halter is causing behind its ears, this does not mean
that animal is simply bored. For instance, its reaction to
buck probably has more to do with its instinctive fear. The
foal's fleeing instinct is activated by the pressure from
behind its ears. It is trying to resist by bucking, and you
should appreciate this. Do not punish the foal, but keep
pressure on its halter rope until it comes closer to you and
relaxes the pressure on its ears by itself. Reward the animal abundantly and walk another few steps forward.
Remember: as long as the foal is standing on its hind legs
the pressure on the rope should not be decreased, but let
the rope relax immediately when it is standing on all fours
again.
Never let the halter rope suddenly slacken when the foal is
standing on its hind legs; you can predict the result for
yourself. A horse can damage its back and neck seriously

and irrecoverably when it falls over backwards. If its back and neck are undamaged, its trust will still be severely dented.

Playfulness

Bucking can also be a sign of playfulness, but it should not be encouraged. Let the foal know that displaying its happiness in this way is not appreciated. It may seem nice to behold such a happily bucking foal, but when the animal develops this into a habit you will have a "happy" bucking horse for the next three years and then his behavior will no longer seem so nice. Be careful of the swinging front legs and keep out of reach of the sharp hooves. Accept that a foal can have crazy moods, but always try to stay put. It is wise to let the foal learn at a young age that it should behave itself in your presence.

The foal is running quickly ahead

Foals are playful and full of life and the playfulness is often uttered in wild behavior. However, the animal will learn that it has to adjust its speed. When the foal runs past you quickly it is best to let the halter rope go somew-

Counter pressure

hat slack, until it is past, and then correct it with a sharp tug on the rope. The foal will learn that it has to stay with you. Ensure that the halter rope is not too stiff and let the rope go slack frequently. Reward the foal when it begins to understand what your intentions are.

If the foal keeps running ahead of you despite the fact that you are correcting it, you can correct it by holding the end of the halter rope or a little whip in front of its face. From here you should send it back to its place; next to you. Try to prevent the animal from walking around you. It is difficult to unlearn such unpleasant behavior. Of course you should never hit it with your hand across the face! You brandish the hand or the whip as a sort of a threat, nothing more.

The trailer

It is a good idea to let the foal get used to the horse trailer. Once it is familiar with the ramp and horse trailer or truck, it will be easier to load it. For the first time, you should load both the mare and the foal together. The foal will not panic as easily when its dam is in the area. It is likely that the foal will refuse the first time you want it to walk up the ramp. The principle that something nice is the best way to persuade it applies here as well. If this does not work, call for help. While holding the foal by the halter rope, ask your two assistants to help you. They have to stand on both sides of the foal and should link arms firmly behind the rear of the foal. In this way you can physically push it into the trailer. If you pick up the hind part of the foal slightly it will be considerably easier to get it in. With a strong foal or big horse, a longeing line can be used behind its backside. It will create a safe distance between the helpers and the horse. Put the animal at ease and praise it when it is standing in the trailer. Give it something to eat as a reward. You should only close the trailer once the animal is at ease. If everything is going well you can even drive the foal a little. Before you drive off though, ensure that everything is well closed. Close the sail or flap well and do not ride with a trailer that cannot be closed on top of the loading ramp. A foal in a panic is capable of clim-

... and that is to walk with willingly

Crazy mood

bing up the loading ramp, and it goes without saying that it could fall out of the trailer in this way. You should of course always drive carefully when you are transporting animals. You should drive, especially on the first ride, at a very slow pace and avoid braking suddenly.

I am learning the most from Mommy

Page 39: Cold blooded horses are calm and courageous

4. In between foal-hood and adulthood

During the period after a horse has been weaned until it is around three years old, it must be able to move around frequently in the open air in full contact with its peers. This is called turning out. It has been proven scientifically that foals that move around a lot on a daily basis grow up to be healthy horses (both physically and mentally) as opposed to their counterparts that are kept in stables all day. Young horses educate each other; a horse is socialized by contact with its counterparts. For this reason you should preferably keep a young horse in the grazing area with its counterparts. If you do not have the space to turn the horse out at your house, you can entrust its care to a horse keeper that specializes in the turning out of young horses. The horses are normally set to graze in fixed groups, preferably with horses of around the same age. The size of the group depends on the size of the pasture and the room available in the stable. In a very limited living area, a horse cannot run away from its counterparts while they are playing. This can be very dangerous.

Movement, outside air and contact with counterparts

Animals must also be isolated from time to time. Colts must of course be kept separately from fillies. The animals

must be inspected daily by the breeder. Discuss this with the person who will be responsible. It is very important that all horses be looked at frequently, and they should preferably be inspected for wounds on a daily basis. A group of young horses are relatively wild and it is not inconceivable that a horse can get injured while playing. Young horses must be fed their additional food separately, and the condition of each individual horse must be carefully checked. The horses must be de-wormed and shoed at the appropriate times. Horses thrive when they are able to make use of a big, safe grazing pasture and roomy roaming stables. Horses that grow thick fur during wintertime should be left like that. The stable will be better suited for them with a light strip between the stable and the pasture. The horses must have sufficient space in the stables to be able to lie down. The floor must be clean and well supplied with straw, for instance.

The size of the group depends on the space available

Turning out at home

You may have enough space at home to keep a few young horses there. This way you can keep frequent contact with the animals. The main advantage of this is that you will be assured that the horses are handled frequently and the training process that has already started as a foal does not come to a standstill for a long period of time. When you turn out

Young horses educate each other

Counterparts the horses at home you must keep at least two young horses together in the pasture. Stimulate the horses to move as often as possible, as movement is very important in the development of a young horse. By simply being on the grass, a horse travels a few kilometers every day. When the horse gets additional exercise by playing with other young horses, it is very likely that it will grow into a healthy horse. Go and walk with the horse regularly. A horse that is confronted with traffic at a young age will experience less stress from it at a later stage. Let the horse get used to the circumstances it is likely to encounter once it is a riding horse; take it into a trailer and make it used to tractors and trucks.

When a horse is about two years old you can take it longeing for the first time. This type of movement is very good for it. Do not overdo it, however. Do not strain the horse with daily longeing sessions. You can also start getting the horse used to a saddle at this age.

Tying up

Ensure that you choose a firm halter and a good halter rope. A halter rope with a so-called panic hook is recommended when you want to tie up your horse. A panic hook is a closing between the rope and halter that can be pulled loose in one yank by the horse in case of panic. A young horse that is experiencing its head being tied up for the first time will resist by hanging on the halter rope in an effort to

Panic hook

pull itself loose. A panic hook will prevent serious damage to the horse, halter or surroundings. Make sure that when you are leading the horse that you are holding it by the halter rope and not the panic hook. An unexpected yank at the halter rope will then undo the panic hook. Check the panic hook before every use; some closing parts will become undone by pulling it quickly at the halter rope.

Bucking

Bucking can be a display of being happy with life, but it can also be resistance. If the animal keeps bucking despite you putting pressure on the halter rope and it has not been convinced to cooperate, we certainly can call this resistance. If your horse has learnt this habit you run the risk that the horse will resist by bucking every time you want it to do something it does not want to do, or when it considers something too difficult. If this is not punished, the horse will learn to buck to get out of boring jobs and this is certainly undesirable. An adult horse that is bucking can certainly not be pulled back with muscle power. Punish this animal with your voice ("Stop it!") and reward it when it is walking with you.

If your young horse does not want to stop bucking, try this method: a horse that repeatedly bucks because it wants to (or a stallion that is trying to intimidate its boss instead of the mares) may not realize that by doing this it is exposing its most vulnerable body parts to attackers; a horse's stomach (and in the case of a stallion, its testicles) will be unprotected when the horse bucks. A horse that will get a tap on the stomach will get such a fright from the fact that its stomach and testicles have been exposed that it will stop this behavior and probably never repeat it again.

Stepping back

If the relationship between the horse and boss is good, the horse will realize that you are the leader. If you still encounter problems with bucking and it does not want to walk with you then the hierarchy between you and the horse has probably not been well established. It is recommended to work on this first of all before you proceed with the training.

---

5. READY TO BEGIN

When can a horse carry a rider?

There is no definitive guideline for when a horse is ready to carry a rider. This depends strongly on the mental as well as physical development of the horse. Most breeds of horses can be broken in at the age of around three, but a slightly built, small animal that still displays a lot of foal-like behavior should be left until around fall time in its third year or even springtime of its fourth year. On the other hand, a big riding horse with a sufficiently heavy behind and well developed body is often sufficiently mature at the age of two and a half.

Keep in mind that the work can also affect the horse mentally: a very nervous horse that does not yet trust humans sufficiently cannot be broken in until it is men-

A 3 year old "Dutch Warmblood Studbook" horse ready for the start

Arabian horse

tally ready for it. Most breeds of horses are only complete-ly mentally and physically mature at around seven.

Maturing late

Some breeds, such as the Arabic and Icelandic horses, mature later and cannot be broken in at the age of three.

Taking it out of the pasture

You have come this far. Your horse has been taken out of the place where it was turned out. The valuable time it spent during the turning out with the other young horses in the grazing pastures can be called "training" in itself. It has been educated widely by its counterparts, is mentally trai-ned and socialized. It has been reprimanded and rewarded by the other horses and is now physically mature enough to be reprimanded and rewarded by you. In the meantime the animal has been frequently handled and made sufficiently halter tame. We will assume that the animal has not been longed and it is not familiar with the saddle or bridle. You are taking it out of the pasture as a three-year-old and want to prepare it to become a riding horse.

Polish

Once again, give the horse enough opportunities to get used to you. An anxious young horse must first of all be convin-

ced that you do not mean it any harm and that your presence does not have bad consequences for it. Groom the horse while softly speaking to it. Start by grooming the neck and breast, preferably with a soft brush. After this you can carefully groom the legs. Be careful when the horse is really anxious, but let it know that you are its boss; do not tolerate any dominant behavior.

Before you can start with the training the animal must willingly allow you to touch it all over, also under the stomach and on the head. The latter has to do with the putting on of the bridle, but also because you must be able to tie and untie it from the longeing line when longeing. It must also be possible to pick all four of the horse's feet up one by one.

Polish

It is possible that the horse can stand on the line during longeing, and you must be able to get the line out from under it.

"Foot up"

A young horse will not immediately understand when it has
to pick up which foot if it has not been trained frequently
to do it. Use the command "foot up" when the horse has to
give you its foot. Start with the left front foot, because a
horse must always be approached from the left hand side.
You should also always get on a horse on the left side. Stand
next to the left front leg of the horse with your back facing
its head. Take it by the knee. Give it the command "foot
up" and pull the leg up. If the horse does not lift its foot
from the ground, push with your left shoulder against the
left shoulder of the horse. This will put the horse off balance a bit which will enable you to lift the leg. Support the
hoof well. If the horse is not used to this, do not lift the foot
too high or for too long. Needless to say, you do not need to
put the foot back down on the ground again. Next you must
lift the left hind leg, followed by the right front and the
right hind leg. If the horse begins to fall more or less against
you, you should let the leg go and quickly move out of the
way. If the horse nearly falls over it will most probably look
for support against you next time. If the horse is resisting by
pulling the leg back down or moving its leg quickly to and
fro, do not give in and try to hold the foot. Punish and
reward the horse with your voice. Only in this way will it
learn that resistance is futile. If the horse becomes aggressive while you are picking up the hind leg, call for help: a kick
from a horse can kill a person.

"Down"

It can be irritating if the horse picks up its leg while it is
being groomed, its legs are being washed or leg protectors
are being put on its leg. For this reason it is recommended
that you teach the horse the command "down!" The horse
will clearly learn the difference between picking up and
putting down its feet.

"Back" and "move"

The command "back" is of immense value not only in the
stable, but also when the horse has been broken in and you

want it to move backwards under the rider. To teach it this command, push the horse to the back while saying "back." The horse will understand at some point what you mean and it will take a few steps back by itself upon hearing the command "back."

The command "turn" is used when you want the horse to move a bit to the left or the right (like when it is standing on your foot for instance!). "Move" can be taught in the same way; that is by pushing the horse while saying "move." The commands "back" and "move" form a very important part of its education: a well educated horse will make space for its boss and a good boss will teach this to his/her horse. When the horse trusts you, is at its ease in your presence and knows the commands "move," "back," "foot up" and "down," you can start with further training.

"Lift foot"

At ease in your presence

"Back"

6. LONGEING

Longeing

To make the horse even more used to you, your voice and the hierarchical relationship between you and it, we will start with longeing. As soon as the animal gets used to the principle of longeing, you can start making it used to a saddle and bridle to refine the longeing. In this way you will enable the horse to quietly soak up all of the impressions. Take your time and only expose the horse to something new once it has become accustomed to what it has already been shown.

Longeing circle

It goes without saying that a horse can longe more easily in a longeing circle than out in the open field. If the animal

Longeing circle has a wide open space around it the temptation to break out is often very great – an intelligent horse picks up bad habits much quicker than it can unlearn them. You should therefore longe in a closed-off longeing circle. If you do not have a longeing ring, a part of the riding area or grazing pasture must be closed off for the purpose. This can be done with obstacle poles, colored tires or ropes, obstacle rails or bails

of straw. A temporary longeing circle could have the disadvantage of slippery grass, which can frighten an inexperienced horse. If there is slippery grass, fill the running area in the longeing circle with sand or sawdust. You should also be careful that the top layer of the longeing circle is not loose. It is very bad for the horse's hooves and joints to struggle through heavy sand for a long time. The diameter of the longeing circle should be around 14 yards.

With a halter there is less control throughout

Show halter: not suitable for longeing

Caveson

A good way to teach a horse how to longe is with a caveson. Approximately speaking, a caveson is a halter with a reinforced nose strap. There are three rings on the nose strap. The longeing line must be tied to the foremost nose band (on the back of the horse's nose). The eventual assisting headstall can – later on – be tied to the rings that are tied to the sides. The advantages of a caveson are:

- The horse is easier to control than with a halter because the longeing line is fixed to the front and the firm nose band puts pressure on the head. A horse that is not used to being longed can easily escape from a halter on a longeing line.
- A caveson is made from sturdier material than a headstall.
- The horse does not need to have a bit yet. This is the case when a horse is being longed on a headstall. Because the horse is not yet used to the bit during this phase of the training it would not be nice to introduce a learner to a bit at this stage. This should only be done with more experienced horses.
- A bit can be added to the caveson later on. A horse can get used to the feeling of a bit in its mouth without having the pressure if the bit exerted on it.

Always pay careful attention when putting on the caveson that the nose strap is at least at the height of two fingers away from the cheekbone and that the nose strap connects well on the nose.

Longeing line

Pay attention to the quality of the longeing line. The sliding hook must be big and sturdy and the line itself must be properly stitched. You should buy a longeing line with a length of around 10 yards. A longer one is not useful, because this will put the horse out of your reach. On top of that, you will

*In further
training the
whip remains
an important
accessory; make
sure that the
horse will not
associate negative
experiences
with it*

also have much more line "left" in a longeing circle with a diameter of 14 yards. With a too-short line, the horse will be forced to walk in a too-small circle. This is also bad for your wrists and side. A longeing line must slide easily through the hands of the person doing the longeing if the length is being increased. There are longeing lines made from nylon available. If you care about your hands, do not use these. If the horse gives the line a firm tug it will burn you right through your gloves. Buy a line made from cotton or linen instead.

Longe whip

The longeing whip is an absolute necessity during longeing. Take note: the whip is NOT to hit the horse with. The longe whip serves as a replacement for the urging of the (rider's) legs; to urge the horse forwards, in other words. During longeing the horse can be gently touched with the whip. Cracking a longeing whip may be nice in the circus, but you will only scare the horse with it here. Instead, buy a soft whip with a length of minimally six and a half feet. In a good whip, the snare (the long rope) is longer than the whip. Before you go longeing, make sure that the horse gets used to the whip beforehand. The aim of the whip is not to scare the animal. Some horses have unfortunately had negative experiences with whips from their younger days.

Leg protectors

Because it is not inconceivable that a young horse will caper around a bit while longeing, you should not longe without leg protectors. You can choose from:

• **Tendon guards**

These serve as protection for the bending tendons on the front legs. A tendon guard must fit well and attached so that it closes at the back.

• **Stud guard**

To protect the horse from kicking its own rear legs. The stud guard works well when it is in position with the thick part on the inside and the closing part showing towards the back.

• **Leg protectors**

Leg protectors that are tightly fastened to the legs protect against injuries when the horse kicks itself. Leg protectors must fit well. There are leg protectors for the front and the hind legs.

• **Bandages**

Elastic winding offers special firmness. If you use a bottom layer it will also protect the horse's sensitive legs against injuries. Only use bandages that will stay 100% secured while you are working: the horse can (and probably will) become panicky when a loose bandage is flying around. The results of a horse that goes to stand on a loose bandage cannot be forgotten. For this reason you should put an additional strip over the knot or closing piece that is on the bandage. Be careful that the bandage is not wound too tightly around the leg as this will hamper the blood flow.

Tendon protector

> **Fear**
> Some horses become very scared when they are wearing leg protectors for the first time. Understand this and allow the animal some time to get used to the strange feeling around its legs.

Assistant

Once again: the indispensable assistant. When the horse is taken to longe for the first time, it is much easier if someone is there to lend a helping hand. Let your assistant walk with the horse by hand around the circle with you standing in the middle. This will prevent you from having to physically persuade the horse to walk the first time. The first longeing lesson can be very calm with the assistant. First of all, let the animal walk around to the left: this is the easiest side for most horses. The assistant must put the horse at ease and teach it how to start. The aim is for the horse to slowly move its attention from the assistant to you and that it should learn how to listen to your advice. It goes without saying that you should only work with someone who has experience working with young horses. An anxious assistant will do more harm than good.

Why longe?

Some people only longe to release a horse from its "stable tiredness," or rather to let a fresh horse that just came out of the stables "stretch its legs" and let it move a bit. Longeing can also be used to make a horse saddle tame and let it get

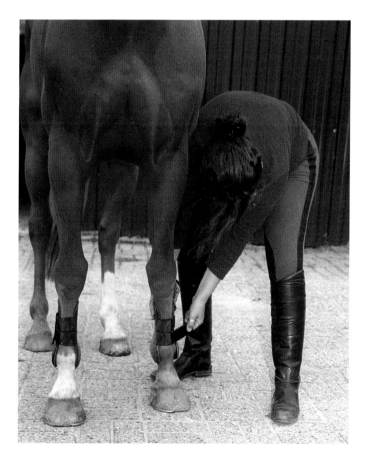

Give it time to get used to the strange feeling around its legs

The indispensable assistant

used to the bit and commands. First and foremost it is for the horse to get used to voice commands, and later to the reins, saddle and the slight pressure of the bit. In addition, the (future) rider can get a good idea while longeing of the capabilities of the horse and any eventual behaviors the horse may display while longeing is perfected. Longeing is a good way to make a horse relax.

Pay attention:
- Try to ensure that the animal relaxes sufficiently so that longeing can begin while it is walking. If the horse storms away wildly, it can injure itself. If necessary, let it loose in the pasture for a while.
- If the horse is very tense during longeing, it is a good idea to allow it to rest the next day. This will be good for the physical and mental well-being of the horse.
- The best way to reward a horse that is working well is to let it graze or go back to the stable.

The purpose
Start walking to the left while holding the whip lightly in your right hand. The rope part should show towards the tail of the horse with the whip in the up position. The longeing

1: Take note of the horse's posture; the head is held too high here. The back is pushed away and the hind legs are picked up behind. There is too much tension

2: The tension is reducing; you can see that the gaze of the horse is becoming less suspicious

3: The horse is walking relaxed forward-down-wards. It is in balance and places its hind legs under its body mass. You should strive for this when longeing

Starting to walk calmly

The whip, longeing line and horse form a triangle

line, whip and horse must form a triangle; you will literally be locking up the horse between the whip and longeing line. Do not walk with the horse, but stay put in the middle. Let the assistant walk next to the horse if the horse does not understand what is happening. The longeing line must be attached to the caveson or halter so that you will have light contact with the horse's head; there should be slight tension on the longeing line. The folds of the longeing rope must be held in your left hand with each fold around the same length so that you can let it go gradually.

Increasing the tempo

As soon as the horse realizes that the circle keeps running around you, you can start making it used to your voice and whip commands. Give it the command "forward" to let the horse walk away. If you want the horse to start trotting, give it the command "trot" and to gallop the command "gallop." Keep increasing the tempo while giving the commands, with the whip horizontally behind the horse. Touch it softly with the whip on the back if it does not understand the command you gave it. Many people make clicking sounds with their tongues to increase the pace. Once the horse has learnt this you do not need to touch it with the whip anymore.

Reducing the tempo

To reduce the trot to a walk, or from a gallop to a trot, give it the command "whoa" while indicating with the whip to the shoulders of the horse. It is extremely important that the horse understands that the command "whoa" means that it should reduce the pace. The horse will most probably not understand at first what it should do. To do this you should apply more force to the head of the horse. Do not yank the longeing line, but increase the pressure on

The posture is still somewhat stressed here

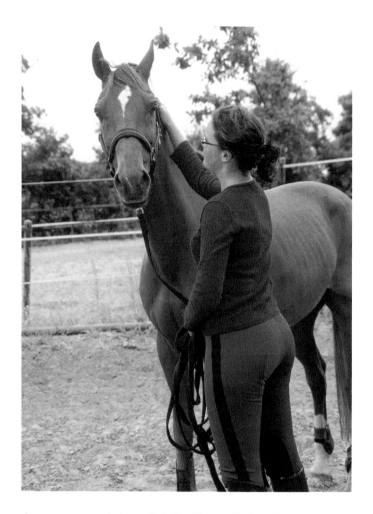

the caveson or halter slightly. You will then be creating a semi-delay, so to speak. On the saddle, a semi-delay means that the rider will be holding the horse back with the help of the reins (see chapter 9).

Coming to a halt

To stop completely, use the command "halt" and teach the horse that it must stop when receiving the command. It is essential to teach it this. The horse may only approach you when you give it the command "come here." You should then tuck the whip under your arm with the rope part facing away. When you approach the horse it is also wise not to point the whip at the horse. The best way to ensure that a horse will come to you is by rewarding it abundantly. This can also be handy when the horse is difficult to catch in the pasture.

Longeing problems: starting off too hard

Many horses will start running very fast with the first touch of the longeing whip, or simply due to stress or malice. If the horse does not react to the previously mentioned methods, try to make the longeing line shorter. Keep shouting the command "whoa" while doing this. If this does not help it is better to turn things around; the horse should now be rewarded and if it begins to slacken the tempo you should punish it. Put the horse to work, keep contact with its head and lock the body between the whip and longeing line. After a while the horse will definitely want to decrease the tempo but it should only be allowed to do this after you have given the command. The idea behind this is for it to keep running until it does not like the idea anymore. It is easier to keep a horse at a certain pace with the longeing line than to let it decrease the pace. We are of course assuming that there is no panic involved and that you will give it the command to walk when you can see that the horse is really getting tired.

Longeing problems: breaking out

Some horses begin to hang on the longeing line and literally pull the person to the outside. Try to correct the animal with a semi-delay. When the animal keeps hanging on the longeing line at the exit because it wants to run back out again (remember that every horse will quickly learn where the exit is) you can put an obstacle rail on the ground or ask the assistant to set up a place for the horse to walk through.

Too hard for the beginning. Always keep a bit of tension on the longeing line!

Longeing problems: coming to the middle

When your horse is threatening to come to the middle, try to keep the slight contact you have with the head by taking your "longeing hand" to your hip. Send the horse back out with assistance of the whip: point the whip towards the horse's middle and touch it – if it is necessary – on the middle or back side with the whip. Ensure that the horse will keep up its tempo. Teaching it the command "go away" will help ensure that the horse will know to keep moving.

Longeing problems: the horse is turning around

Once the horse has learnt that the longerer is relatively powerless when the horse is standing right in front of him/her, it will be difficult to unlearn this behavior. Ensure that the horse maintain a sufficient pace. If you can see that the horse is too busy moving to come and stand in front of you, move your body so that you will be slanted behind the horse, in the direction of its hind legs. Like this, you can let it keep moving with the help of the whip – and quick reactions. If you are not fast enough you can call in the help of an assistant. The assistant can run on the outside with the horse. Some horses will try to turn by stopping the back hand of the longerer and thereby turning the front hand to the back. Keep facing the shoulder of the horse and try to keep the horse on the inside with the forehand. You can keep the backside of the horse to the outside with the help of the whip. If this is not working, let the horse walk with its backside against the longeing line. Keep the line low enough so that it cannot walk underneath it. Be careful

Turning around: often a case of reaction possibilities

when the horse is turning its backside to you; an accident is about to happen.

Longeing problems: The horse is turning around and kicking

If a horse turns around and kicks at you, you can punish it with the whip as this is extremely dangerous behavior. Be firm but fair, and try to determine why the horse is reacting like this. The line between resistance through malice or resistance through fear and a lack of understanding is often not clear. The trainer should judge whether the horse must be punished, or if it is not mentally ready for the work and simply does not understand what is required of it.

Jumping

7. Getting used to the saddle and bridle

Getting used to the saddle

The first time a saddle is placed on a horse's back, it can get frightened. Prepare the horse for what is coming. Stroke it firmly on the back while you talk to it calmly. It is better to do this in the stable: a horse feels more relaxed in a trusted environment. The risk of saddling the horse while it is standing loose in the stable is that it can damage the (often expensive) saddle. To prevent this you have to tie the horse up, but this has a disadvantage as well: the horse can feel tied in and react anxiously. Only do this if the horse is used to being tied up. Another possibility is to put a single saddle pad with a longeing sheath on the back. Do this even if the horse is nervous and gets quickly scared by new expe-

Longeing sheath

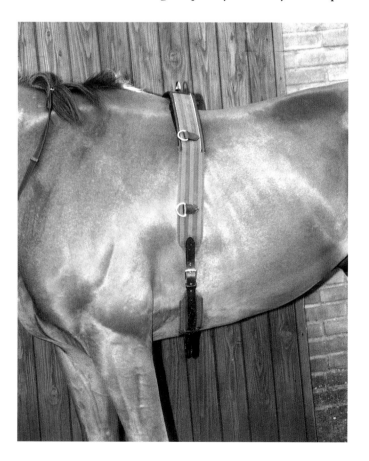

riences. For preference, use an elastic longeing sheath. If the animal walks away when you want to put the saddle on, ask your assistant to keep the animal in position in the stable. Make sure that the rings are sticking up so that you can tie it with the ring straps to the saddle.

Saddling up

For breaking in you should preferably use an old saddle, if you have one. More important than lifetime or price tag of the saddle is whether it fits well, of course. A saddle that does not close well on the back of the horse will cause pain and fear (with all of the negative consequences) especially when there is a rider sitting on it. Lay the saddle carefully on the horse's back with the front part a bit higher up on the withers and move it gently to the back. Let the saddle stay there for a bit and put the horse at ease before you put on the sheath. Do not tie the sheath too firmly at first. Depending on the reaction of the horse, you may or may not be able to proceed with the saddling. If the animal is greatly influenced by the experience, it is better to let it stand in the stable with the saddle on – but stay out of its vicinity.

Correctly tied rings

English nose strap

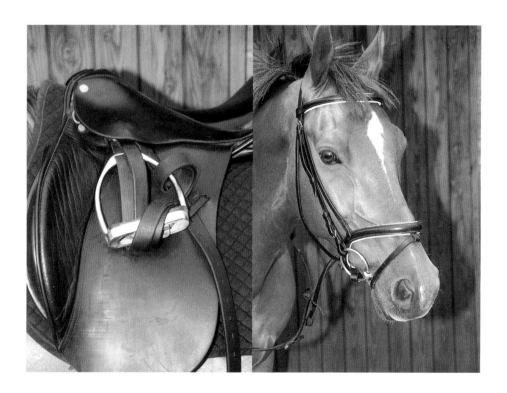

Tie the longeing line to the caveson or halter and walk with the animal at hand through the longeing circle. Start the longeing – as always – with a walk. Try to prepare the animal in this way so that it will not go jumping around wildly because of the saddle on its back. This can have negative results for both the horse and the saddle. If the horse is scared nevertheless, try to calm it with your voice. You should always keep calm yourself; the horse will see from your reaction whether you are still in control of the situation. Do not longe too long for the first time. Stop as soon as the horse shows understanding and has accepted the saddle.

Bridle

Getting used to the headset should not present any insurmountable problems. The horse is used to the halter already, after all. Always use the reins. A combination nose strap (English nose strap with a blocking strap) is usually used, or a (low) training nose strap.

Bridle and bit

The feeling of the bit in the mouth will be a complete new experience for the horse. There are only a few types of bits that are suitable for training a horse. Never use a rod (unbroken bit) or a correction bit with an inexperienced horse. The bit should not be too heavy either, because it would dig into the horse. A too-thin bit would be too sharp, but the bit cannot be too wide either; the horse would not be able to close its mouth properly. The bit must stick out around 0.4 inches on either side of the mouth. The most suitable is a doubly-broken rod, because this is the friendliest to the horse's mouth as the pressure in the mouth is divided between the bars (the toothless part of the horse's mouth) and the tongue. A singly-broken rod is also suitable, but it presses a bit more on the bars. You can choose between the following types of bits:

- **Jointed eggbutt**
The mouth corners of the horse are protected because this mouth piece is strapped to the bit ring through "pipes."
- **D bit**
The bit rings are in the shape of a D. The advantage of this bit is that it cannot be drawn through the horse's mouth. It is lying relatively freely in the mouth.

- **French link eggbutt**
The round bit rings run through the bars at the ends of the mouthpiece. This bit is suitable for a young horse, but it is better to protect the mouth corners with rubber rings.

Getting used to the bit

A common method to get the horse used to the bit is to loosen the bit on one side. The bit will be hanging on one cheek piece while the bridle is being put on. It should then be put very carefully through the mouth and tied to the cheek piece. The disadvantage of this method is that you must fidget with the horse's head during this new experience. If you are sufficiently experienced, rather fasten the bridle. The horse will undoubtedly refuse to open its own mouth when you hold the bit in front of it. The quickest way to let the horse enjoy the bit is by dipping a moist bit in some sugar or bread crumbs. In this way its first confrontation with the cold, hard object in its mouth will be a pleasurable experience. The horse will quickly learn that it is

Jointed eggbutt

D bit

French link eggbutt

*Support the bit
with the right
hand*

*Careful over
the eyes*

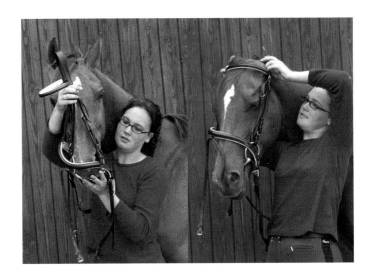

wise to hold its mouth open when you have the bit in front of it. The nice parts must be left out at a later stage, of course. Take care that the bit does not hit the teeth as you put it in. Support the bit with your right hand while your left hand, with the cheek straps in it, is resting on the bridge of the horse's nose. You should only leave the bit in the horse's mouth when it used to the feeling (and it has tasted the sugar) and then tie the throat strap and nose strap in. Do not grab the horse firmly by the reins when you take it to the outside. The first time the bit will put some pressure on its mouth the horse will get a fright. You can also make the horse used to the bit by adding a bit to the caveson. The bit will then be hanging in the mouth without any pressure being exerted on it. In this way the horse can calmly nibble on the bit while it is busy longeing and accept the bit in a relaxed manner.

Longeing on the bit with the bridle

Never tie the longeing line to the inside bit ring, because the bit can be pulled through the horse's mouth in this way. The trust of the horse – which is so very important – will not be promoted in this way. It is much better to tie the longeing line to the bit ring on the inside, as well as the nose strap. In this way the pressure will be divided between two firm parts of the nose strap and the inner mouth corners. Put the sliding hook firstly through the bit ring and under the nose strap. Tie the sliding hook to the rope next. When changing hands the line must then be tied to the other side

of the bit ring. Later, when the horse is more experienced –
the longeing line can eventually be tied to an in-between
piece (which connects the bit rings with each other), or if
you are making use of assisting reins, directly on the bit
rings. The disadvantage of the in-between piece is that the
pressure is being directly exerted on the mouth of the horse.
Do not forget to fasten the reins. The horse can get a fright
from the flapping reins and can even stand on them. A
good way to prevent this is to simply put the reins over the
neck and tie it to the throat strap. Wind the reins once
together and then tie it to the throat strap.

Adding the bridle
It is wise to let the horse get used to the pressure of the bit
before you actually ride it. A good way to do this is by
"adding" to the horse. Once the horse has learnt how to
longe you can make it used to the added reins or assisting

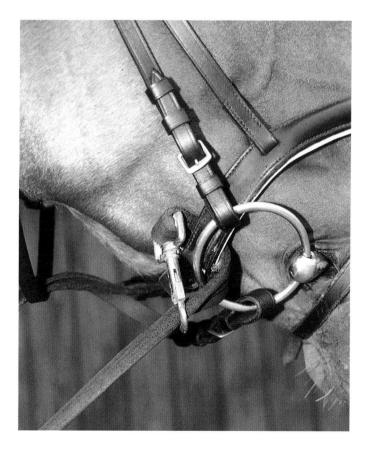

*Longeing line
tied to the inner
bit ring and nose
strap*

In-between piece

reins. Except for the fact that the horse will have the pressure of the bit on both sides the conduct of the horse can also be improved. A suitable way to add to a young horse is with assisting reins, or simply with strings that connect the bit rings with the longeing strap or the saddle. Because we view the addition in this phase as a way to make the horse used to the bit, we will not discuss all the different ways of adding.

Added reins

Gogue

Strings

The biggest advantage of using a cord (of which the Dutch horse trainer Lammert Haanstra is the "inventor") is that you do not need to add the precious assisting reins or a gogue. If all goes well you will only need these aids during longeing. A good rider must be able to keep the horse in the correct position with a saddle and ride it in a relaxed way without assisting reins.

Tying in of the added reins

Do not put the added reins or strings on in the stable. First of all, longe the animal in the usual way and then – in the longeing circle – tie the added reins. To ensure that the horse is bent in the correct way – in its stride it must be somewhat bent in so that it is looking in the direction in which it is going – make the inner added rein a fraction shorter that the outer one. The added reins should not be tightened too much the first time; the animal must be able

Strings between the front legs

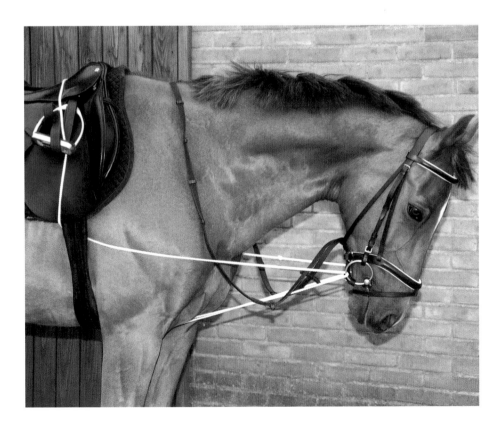

to keep its nose ahead of the lead line and be able to lower its head. Too loose is not good either; nothing must be flapping. If you want to use a string, use a cord with a length of around twenty feet. Tie a knot in the middle. The knot must be placed on the saddle peak. A suitable way to add to the horse is to put the rope through the stirrups and tie it under the sweating pad to the sheath. From this point run the rope to the bit rings, then through the bit rings through the front legs of the horse again and then to the sheath. You can also tie the rope from the stirrups to the bit ring and from there attach it to the sheath again just under the sweat pad. Judge for yourself what the horse is accepting and with which method it is the most relaxed when longeing. Keep the horse on track and prevent panic by not asking for too much ("over-demanding") and be careful that the horse does not become stressed.

*Strings under
the sweating pad*

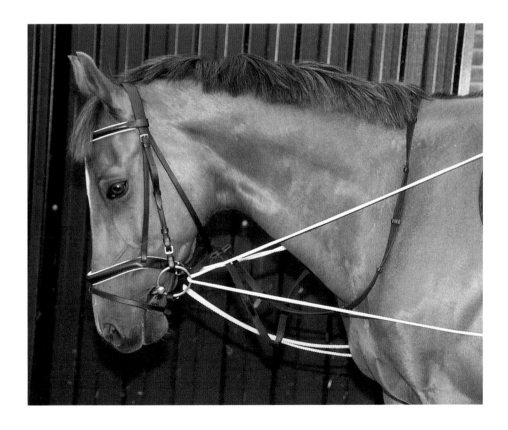

Posture

The first aim is to get the animal to the stage where it can longe in a relaxed manner. This means that it will be walking forward-downwards while the longerer keeps contact with the horse's mouth. This means that the horse does not lift its head, but stretches its neck. By doing this the muscles in the top neck (under the mane) are tensed and this relaxes the bottom part of the neck. A horse that is upright and is hereby burdened in an incorrect manner, will be tensing its muscles at the bottom of its neck. It will develop a so-called "swan neck" in this way. During the forward-downwards walking the back muscles are working in a good way. The back is making a ball when the horse is walking in the incorrect manner and where it is pushing its back away it truly forms a hollow point. When the entire manner of the horse from its ears to its tail root shows a slight curve, the horse is bringing its hind leg under the mass, whereby the back part of the body is "propelled"; with a horse that is running well, the back part is the driving part! A horse that does not move through the back in a relaxed manner is making smaller strides with its hind legs and is tilting its lead joints in the direction of the tail root with its lead joints too far under its stomach to be able to run "well."

More tension; the horse is pulling away a bit

Perfecting the longeing

If you are experienced with longeing you can longe the horse on a double line to make it used to the one-sided pressure of the reins. In this way you can teach the horse, before you even start riding it, how it will be steered. Working with a double longeing line is a good way to perfect the longeing, but only if either the horse or the longerer, and preferably both, are sufficiently experienced. The feeling of a longeing line running behind the back can cause stress in a young horse; you can imagine for yourself what could happen if a horse becomes panicky with a double longeing line. An experienced person knows how the horse can react and anticipates this. An inexperienced person should first try and perfect the art of longeing with an experienced horse. Even an experienced person should use an assistant when longeing with a double line though, to be able to offer assistance if it is required.

Good posture. The horse is walking relaxingly forward-downwards

8. RIDING FOR THE FIRST TIME

When is the horse ready to be ridden?

If a horse has gone through the above-mentioned phase of the training with confidence, it is ready for the next step. This can be taken if the horse satisfies the following criteria:

- It is walking in a relaxed way forward-downwards on the longeing line, as well as running to the left and the right and walking, trotting and galloping.
- It seems friendly. The ears are pointy while it is working.
- It accepts the bit. You will recognize this on a closed mouth, as well a horse that is frequently nibbling on the bit. It is a good sign if the mouth is slightly frothing. The person has slight contact with the mouth of the horse and the horse is reacting calmly when he/she causes a slight hold back.
- It accepts the saddle. The back is not being pulled back, but the horse is walking smoothly with all of the body. The tail is held slightly relaxed; a wildly swinging tail is a sign of resistance.
- The pace is regular. The legs are being picked up robustly and firmly and rhythmically put down again. The horse obeys forward and does not slouch. The backside is driving the body forward. The back leg is

Friendly and relaxed

*Forward-
downwards*

visibly placed under the mass.
- The horse is galloping to the left and the right calmly and relaxed and jumps to a good gallop.
- The voice commands are familiar. The horse reacts well to the command "forward," "canter," "gallop," "whoa," "halt" and "come here." The command "whoa" is of special importance. It provides proper mental calmness to the rider, who can be confident that the horse will reduce its pace when the command is given.

Stable bravado

Energy: attention points

Even though the horse must be well advanced and in perfect condition, it is not a good idea to overload the horse with power food. Give it a lot of grass and rough food and be stingy with the protein-rich briquettes and oats, for instance. A calm horse is easier to ride and it is a shame if you have to "fight against your own fodder," as it is said. Ensure that the horse is relieved from its stable courage. A horse that walks in the pasture frequently will behave more calmly than an animal that is kept in a stable all day. Some owners of precious race horses do not let their horses go into pasture by preference, because the horse can injure itself while playing. These horses are trained more times per day in general and will never be left in the stable 24 hours per day. It is a heavy mental and physical burden for a young

Every horse will be happier if it can walk around in the pasture for a few hours a day

horse to have to work more than once a day. It is better to give it frequent rest days. A horse will feel happier if it can walk in the pasture for a few hours every day and get rid of its energy. It will display its gratitude for this while you are riding it.

Weight

I personally do not believe that a horse should get used to a weight on its back before a rider climbs in the saddle. The animal already knows the feeling of the saddle on its back. If the saddle is being made heavier with weights it is a dead weight, which is a very different experience than a moving rider. Do not experiment with dummies or bags of hay: the horse will never understand the link between a rider and a wildly shaking object on its back. It is impossible for a dummy to follow the movements of a horse and it will only cause panic and fear. It will be a real shame to have built up the confidence of the horse and then damage it in this way.

Safety first!

Hopefully you will be wise enough to protect yourself. The saying "it will never happen to me" has already led to some very serious accidents.

• Fencing

Look at the area you plan to ride in with a critical eye. A wooden divide longeing circle is well-suited to longeing,

This horse clearly has some energy left

*Make sure
that you have
a good fence*

**Safety first:
Safety and boots**

but not to ride a young horse in. A horse that is running flat out creates a sort of centrifugal result. In this way, a falling rider will always be thrown to the outside. This will therefore create an extraordinary good chance of the rider falling heavily against the wooden fencing. Longe the horse when the horse is being ridden for the first time, preferably in a safe environment. If the riding area is also camped off with wood it is best to do it in the middle of the riding area.

• **Helmet**

While riding a horse you should always, even more so during training, wear an approved, well fitting and firm

Buck strap

safety helmet. The old-fashioned cap that is held in position by an elastic band is absolutely insufficient for this purpose. A good safety helmet is not only a cover for the head, but can be life-saving protection. The helmet must always be in position and be firm and undamaged. Ask for advice at a good riding outlet.

- **Riding boots**

Laced shoes and profile soles are not suitable. Many serious accidents have happened due to a rider falling and his/her shoes getting stuck in the stirrups. Rather use standard riding boots. Except for the fact that the soles are smooth, the shaft of the boots also protects your lower legs.

- **Further protection**

There are special body protectors available to protect the middle of a rider during a fall. Wearing one is not an unnecessary luxury.

Buck strap

A buck strap is a mounting ring strap that is tied around the neck of the horse, in the direction of the shoulders. The rider can look for support on this strap, instead of using the reins for this purpose. Longe the horse with the buck strap around its neck first of all and only mount it once it is used to it.

Mounting

Longe the horse in the way it is used to it, and then ask your assistant to hold the horse. For your own safety it is best to put the horse's head in a corner of the manger or facing towards a fence. Climbing into the saddle in the stable is very dangerous, and this also goes for the area where the horse is tied up. The horse must not feel like it is locked up or tied up, but must simply experience that this is the next logical step in its training. It trusts you and knows that no negative experiences have occurred during the training. The assistant must also be reassuring towards the horse and not scare the animal or hold it too tightly. A vice-grip will only cause stress. It is better not to use the stirrups the first few times. You will then be forced to jump on top of the horse while the bone of your left buttock presses into its rib-

Mounting:
let someone hold
the horse

Mounting rings:
do not dig into
the ribs

Push firmly
on the saddle

Let the assistant
give you a
foothold

cage. There are few people who can be gentle and quiet when climbing in the saddle while using the stirrups for the first time to get on a young horse! Rather stand next to the horse and lay your hand on the saddle. Push firmly on the saddle and in doing so you should put as much of your upper body weight as possible on it. Keep the horse calm and reward it. When it reacts with confidence, ask your assistant to "give you a leg-up." Your assistant should fold their hands into each other around your left ankle and push you gently up, until you are hanging on your stomach over the saddle. Talk to the horse and put it at ease while you stay as calmly as possible in this uncomfortable position. Wait until the horse is standing still calmly. Push yourself up on the stem of the saddle so that you can put your left foot in the mounting ring and put your right leg over the horse. Try not to touch the backside of the horse with your right foot and not to hurt the horse with your left buttock. It is also very important that you land in the saddle very gently. When mounting becomes a bad experience for your horse, you will have problems with it for a long time to come. It will then be very difficult to teach the horse to stand still while you are mounting it.

Nervous

If the horse reacts nervously to the rider hanging with his/her stomach over the saddle, it is best to walk a little with the horse for it to get used to the weight. The advantage of this is that the rider – in case the horse jumps away or starts jumping – will be able to land on his/her feet quickly. However, there is also a disadvantage; in this position, it is not possible to adjust to the movements of the horse and the horse will not become calmer because of this. If the horse goes off running or jumps away, it will be extremely uncomfortable. For this reason, it is best to hang over the saddle a few times first of all with a nervous horse while it is standing still. You should only mount it once it has accepted this and is used to it. Do not forget that it will be even worse for the horse if you are nervous as well. This will not be the case if you are calm and relaxed and radiate this to the horse. If you cannot keep your own nerves under con-

Very comfortable!

trol at this important phase of the training, you are probably not experienced enough to train the horse further. If the longeing and mounting take too long and you get the impression that you are asking too much of the horse, it is best to reward the horse and let it go and rest. Keep the "real" ride for next time.

The first steps

If the horse stays calm and accepts your weight, sit calmly and firmly in the saddle. Put your legs gently against the horse. Be careful; do not push or drive the horse, simply put your legs next to its body. Try not to push with your calves, even if the horse reacts nervously to the strange expe-

Do not dig
the lower leg in

*Try to prevent
the horse from
jumping forward
anxiously*

rience of being locked between two legs. It is said that a
mare especially can be very much under the influence of
the rider's legs because she experiences a similar feeling
when a stallion mounts her. The front legs of the stallion are
located in approximately the same position during mating.
Show understanding for the feelings of the horse, but get it
to tolerate the feeling of rider's legs against its body.

Next, the rider should give the command "forward" calmly
and increase slightly the pressure of the calves at the same
time. This simply serves as preparation for the steering
commands. It is not intended that the horse should react to
the command from your calves yet, but this will make it
somewhat used to the commands that will come later on.
The assistant must walk along next to the horse, holding it;

the longeing line in the left hand and the reins held loosely under the head of the horse with the right hand. The reins must be loose from the throat strap. The horse must not be held tightly. The horse must walk relaxed next to the assistant while the rider is holding on to the buck strap, holding the reins lightly. It is sufficient to walk for the first time; do not overdo it. Use your voice to set the horse at ease if it wants to trot or run away. The rider must stay as relaxed as possible and adjust her movements as much as possible to those of the horse. In this way the rider's weight is not seen as a threat, but as an obvious experience.

It is also possible that the horse can be so much under the influence of the experience that it will not want to walk. The weight of the rider will only increase the uncertainty of the horse. Most horses walk for the first time with a rider on their back as if they are walking on eggs, and have a lot of problems maintaining balance. If the horse keeps standing, the assistant should try to get the horse to move with vocal commands and clicking sounds from the tongue. The rider must also tap the horse slightly with the hand or longeing whip on the backside. If this does not work, try to mobilize the horse by having the assistant give it commands from the back or use the longeing whip (do not hit, but

The horse is pulling its back away; the cause can be a painful back

touch, the same as with longeing) to move. Wait for the rest and try to prevent the horse from jumping forward anxiously.

Jumping

A single jump of joy should not take an experienced rider off-course, especially not if he was clever enough to tie the mounting ring strap under the neck of the horse, so that he can hold onto it. You must also keep in mind that a young horse will not always walk "straight into the harness." Jumping repeatedly is not fun for any rider either. In such a case, try to determine the reason why the horse is jumping. It is not fair to punish a horse when it is in pain or scared. The cause could be a saddle that fits badly, or a painful back due to bad back usage.

Falling

It often happens that a jump of joy is the cause of the first fall. Most horses are intelligent enough to connect the cause and effect. When a jump has no negative consequences for a horse, it will probably try to repeat this behavior. Once you have determined that the horse is indeed jumping again and again with the specific aim of letting the rider fall, it is time to take action before this behavior gets any worse. In fact, every bad bit of behavior from the horse that is not consequently tackled in the right way can develop into a serious problem. Punish the horse when it keeps jumping.

The best way to punish the horse is while it is jumping or directly afterwards. When too much time passes between the punishable behavior and the punishment, the horse will never link the punishment with the behavior, and the rider will not achieve anything. A tap with the whip during or directly after the jump will sometimes just make the horse jump harder, and this is not always the best for the rider. Try therefore to first of all calm the horse down by loudly shouting "whoa." If this does not help, you will have to use the whip.

Walking
is important

Walking

At first you should keep to walking with the longeing line, preferably relaxed and forward-downwards. It is also important during further training that the horse warms up for at least 10 minutes by walking. Do not forget to let the muscles cool down afterwards by walking with the long reins after working.

9. RIDER COMMANDS AND RIDING TERMS

From voice commands to rider commands

When the horse is used to the rider on its back, the assistant can take up the task of longeing the horse while the horse is being ridden. Longe the first time with the longeing whip within reach. The horse is already used to this and the idea is for the whip and voice commands used during longeing to now be transformed into rider commands. Strive for relaxation first of all. When the horse starts to trot, the longerer should try to get the horse back to a walk through a voice command ("whoa"), supported by a careful rein command from the rider. The word "whoa" must be familiar to the horse and in this way the command will be transferred to a rider command that is called "delay" or "contain." Because the word "delay" is sometimes associated with "pulling the reins back," the term "causing a delay" is better. By stopping, the so-called "complete containment" is

"Whoa!"

Hollow back

Tilted mouth

caused, during which time the rider must utter the word "halt."

The delay

First of all, we want to teach the horse how to reduce the tempo. This is the delay. Causing a delay is in fact not much more than the rider making him/herself heavy and closing the fingers. In doing this, the rider must place his/her full weight back behind the hip points and tilt the mouth.

During working tempo, the rider must sit on both the hip points with a somewhat hollow back. During a delay the cross should be pulled up, and the mouth tilted, so that the rider will be sitting more to the back of his/her buttocks and thereby making the back less hollow. By locking the fingers, the rider is creating slightly less resistance for the mouth of the horse. The rider is thereby heavier in the saddle and locks his/her fingers, while giving the command "whoa." The command should continue until the horse reacts. The moment the horse slacks the pace (from a walk it means that the horse must come to a halt, and the command "halt" can also be used if the horse knows it) the rider must relax the grip and reward the horse.

Giving in

Giving in means the "position of the hand" (the rider's hand) is not offering any resistance to the horse's mouth and is in smooth contact with the mouth. Giving in does not

mean letting the reins go. When giving in the calves should stay in an unchanged position next to the horse's body, so that the pace will stay the same. Giving in in this way is a sign for the horse that it has interpreted your command well and that you are happy with its reaction. Giving in is not always important during training, but it is an indispensable rider assist. The aim of giving in is that the horse will soon become "yieldable." This means that the horse reacts to rein commands from the rider in a supple and loose way. Its jaw and throat relax and the horse wants to bend its neck. The rider will realize that the horse is yieldable when she can ride with only slight tension in the reins or slight contact with the horse's mouth. A yielding horse can then be ridden with the reins (with the head bent down on the lead line). A horse that has not been under saddle for long will not yet be yieldable, but this should be the aim of the rider. Only a rider with a still, gentle hand that is keeping it independent and firm can make a horse yieldable. A horse that is not made yieldable can never walk with a good lean.

Leaning

Leaning means that the horse is looking for contact with the (soft) rider's hand. Leaning and yieldable seem to be connected to each other. Most people think that leaning means not only contact between the rider's hand and the horse's mouth, but also contact between the horse and the rider's legs and the way the rider is sitting. The rider must

be moving smoothly. A horse that is not reacting well to the
rider's calf commands (for instance) will never be looking
to relax against the rider's hand. You will be able to see
from the posture and movements of the horse if it is leaning
well. A horse that is in smooth contact with both of the
rider's hands is walking with good balance. Many people
call this "walking on its own legs." The horse can bring its
hind legs easily under the mass because its back is taking
the weight in the correct way, and it is looking for good
head/neck posture.

Leaning well back

Semi-delay

A semi-delay means that the rider is holding the horse back with the use of the reins and sitting in such a way that the horse is being held back. The semi-delay should not be held on to, but only executed for a short period of time. This happens when the rider locks his fingers while holding the horse forward with his calf command. The tempo at which the horse is walking can hardly change as a result. A semi-delay is mostly used to make a horse pay attention to what is about to come. During this phase of the training the commands are not yet refined to the extent that the horse will recognize a semi-delay and it is only used to reducing the tempo.

Trot

We are only going to trot once the horse is at ease under the rider and reacts well. The horse will probably not run well or in balance in the beginning. Do not do this for too long either. Only later, when the horse is able to move well under the rider's weight, can we work on its yielding, leaning, impulse, tact, posture and bending. In the beginning you should only be riding lightly, and of course on the good leg. This will hinder the horse as little as possible in its movements. For this reason it is best to hold on to the buck strap. In this way you will stay in the saddle more easily if the horse makes an unexpected movement, and you will not need to look for support from the reins.

It must keep walking actively forward, even without the rider pulling the heels up

Loose?

Many horses have problems trotting under a rider, even when their walking is great. They have problems keeping their balance in the run, especially when the floor of the longeing circle or riding area is very loose. In this case it is best to teach the horse further while loose.

Calf commands

The trotting command tells a horse to trot when given the command "trot" with a driving assist from the calves, eventually helped along with the whip. It is very good if the horse trots a few paces, but it is also acceptable if it takes off anxiously. Every forward reaction to your calf command must be rewarded; refining will come later. In the beginning, the horse will most likely fall out of the trot quickly and look for the known walking rhythm. Do not allow this for too long. The idea is to make the horse "ready in the legs." When you notice that the horse is reacting to your calf commands, it is a good idea to make it react to the whip. Once again: every forward movement must be rewarded. If you consequently keep this up, you will have a horse that is reacting fluently to leg commands during further training. "Lazy" horses, or rather horses that do not respond to the

If the horse does not react sufficiently to calf commands, use the whip instead of driving the heels in

legs, are often trained by inconsistent riders who simply kick a little harder to get the horse to trot when the horse does not react to slight pressure. Do not be seduced into doing this. Driving assists (calf commands) must also be taught to the horse along with the voice commands "forward," "trot" and (later on) "gallop." If necessary, the longerer must explain the commands with the use of the whip.

Reins, calf and weight

Riding a horse well is a combination of rein commands, calf commands and weight assists that can only be supported by voice commands. A good rider knows how to give the commands in good measurements and hardly ever uses only one command at a time. For instance, the rein command cannot be used in the correct way without the appropriate weight and calf assists:

• **Reducing tempo**

When creating a delay, the rider prevents the horse from standing completely still by using the supporting calf command and teaching the horse to react to as little rein assistance as possible by making himself heavy in the saddle.

• **Steering**

While turning, the rider has to keep his inner leg on the sheath and the hind leg somewhat back. This will prevent the horse from swinging out or falling away over the shoulder. It must be taught to bend around the inner leg of the rider. Ensure that the calves stay in a good tempo for this. To swerve to the left, the rider has to push his left buttock bone into the saddle, to the right his right buttock bone. This is the weight assist.

- **Increasing tempo**

To let a horse walk at a constant pace the rider must keep his calves against the horse to ensure that the horse will walk well from the back to the front (driving from behind). To increase the tempo the calf command is mostly used, supported by a correct leaning of the rider's hand. The best way to make progress to a faster pace is by preparing the horse with a semi-delay that a command is about to follow, and then giving it the calf command.

Of course it will not go as well the first time as described here. When the first calf command is given, the horse will not simply start to trot smoothly and calmly. In the beginning the voice and whip commands will be unavoidable, but if the horse is taught well it is only a question of time until it understands what is meant and will have sufficient confidence to react calmly to the commands.

Buttock bones?

Go and sit on a hard chair with your hands under your buttocks. The two bones that you will feel are your buttock bones. With them you must regulate the pressure in the saddle. This is called weight assist. Weight assist is not given by moving the upper body, but the lower body.

Impulse

Impulse is the driving work of the back hand. A horse can only walk on impulse when the leg of the rider is sufficiently active and the horse is leaning well.

Steering, adjusting and bending

Adjusting is the movement of the neck and it means a lot because the horse walks in the direction it is looking in. Bending the length means the bending of the entire horse. The entire body must be slightly bent (while riding in full gallop for instance) when turning, with the back legs running in the same tracks as the front legs. Only later, when turning to the side, may the horse move with its front and back legs in a different set of tracks. It is much too early for that now. The first turn must be taken in steps. Ensure that the commands are given calmly and clearly. When turning left the left hand must be taken from the neck, the left buttock bone must be pushed into the saddle and the hind leg

must be placed behind the sheath. The idea is that the horse
is kept in position by the inside of the rider's left leg. The
horse is therefore turning around the inside of the rider's
leg. The first turn will be executed with a lot of adjusting
and bending and with a swinging behind. If the horse
reacts to the first command it is very good and it should be
rewarded abundantly. We are striving to be turning with a
bend with the correct posture when riding, but it is much
too early for that now.

Tact

Tact is the regularity with which the pace is made, in combination with the
impulse. The rider must strive for the horse to be able to execute dressage,
pick the legs up actively and place the hind legs under the mass.
Only a horse that is not being disturbed in the mouth can make a regular
pace.

10. GALLOPING

Going into a gallop

Do not teach the horse how to gallop until it can relax while trotting and be in balance, look to lean and be yieldable. On top of this it must also hold its back in a relaxed manner, even when the rider is putting it through a few paces. Start with riding it lightly, a relaxing working run in the full. You should start with this to the left as well, because it is the easiest side for horses to walk. If you realize that your horse is walking or trotting more easily to the right, then you should start with galloping to the right. To let a horse fall into a gallop, hold the inside of the reins against the neck and set the horse slightly to the inside in the open. Keep the inside leg in its place. Persist and give the voice command "gallop" in combination with a driving calf assist. It is not important yet for the horse to fall into a good gallop or for it to increase on the usual working trot. This is for later. If the horse understands the command for increasing the pace we can teach it how to go over into a gallop (whereby the front leg forces it forward).

Galloping

Galloping under a rider in full speed is a very heavy burden for a young horse. Galloping should not be taught on the longeing line, but in a riding area where the horse can also run on a long line. If the horse starts galloping with the rider while in the longeing area then there is certainly nothing wrong with that. The horse can only do what it is capable of doing, no more. Try to get the horse to run with the correct assistance.

Towards the inside and keep riding lightly

Preparatory gallop: the backside

Start in the full and ride in a light trot. Try to make the horse bend well around your inside leg. Keep the posture to the inside. Try then to push the back to the inside. The rider does this by giving rhythmic pressure with his/her outer leg, which is behind the sheath, when the horse lifts its outer back leg. If the horse brings the backside somewhat in, its outside hind leg will move under the mass. This will make it easier to pick up pace. It is not the aim for the horse to bring its backside to the inside when picking up the pace, but in learning how to gallop well this is not a problem at all.

Preparatory gallop: the front side

Galloping relaxed

Fall away over the outer shoulder

Afterwards, while the horse is trotting and at the moment when the horse picks up its outer front leg, create a semi-delay with the outer hand so that the outer front leg will be reaching less to the front. In this way we will immediately – while going into a gallop – get the inner front leg to reach to the front. Try this a few times, so that the horse will react calmly when you create a gentle delay every now and then with the outer hand, and push the inner hand to the inside.

Preparatory gallop: weight

Stay seated. If it still does not seem as if the horse is relaxing when you stay seated, you should postpone this for as long as possible. If the horse does start to go faster, you can give it weight assistance more easily by staying seated in the saddle. It is self-evident that this can only be done on a relaxed back that is not being pulled away.

Push your weight to the outer buttock bone. In this way the inside leg of the horse is released from its burden and it can start reaching to the front.

When to start going faster?

To make the picking up of the pace easier you can try to do it when leaving the open, in other words where you can follow the hoofbeats. It should be done in this way: to let a horse run with the correct posture and bent in the full, the rider has to place his/her weight to the middle of the buttock bones. To let a horse jump into a good gallop, the rider must rest his/her weight on the outer buttock bone. This is how you do it. You cannot let a horse run well in the full if your weight is resting on the outside. Yet the leg position in the full is ideal for going into the gallop when galloping on the inside; the horse is bent and the inner front leg is literally walking away from the outer leg.

Drive the horse, with the inner leg while galloping

If it gallops it
is the best horse
in the world,
even when it
starts galloping
incorrectly

Finally: going faster

As you leave the full, push the horse with your inner leg to the outside. Push the horse against your outer leg, which is behind the sheath. The horse stays set to the inside in this way, with the back part to the inside. It must therefore be kept bent around your inner leg. As soon as you feel that the horse is being pushed against your outer leg through the constant pressure from your inner leg, push it with your inner leg to a gallop. Make sure that your inner hand stays relaxed and that the outer hand is supported. If the support of the outer hand falls away the horse will start running on the outer shoulder and will therefore start running incorrectly because its weight is brought to the outer front leg. If it starts galloping it is the best horse in the world, even if it starts galloping in the incorrect way.

If it is not working

Do not worry too much about it. There are few horses that never learn how to start galloping well. If your horse keeps starting to gallop in the incorrect way and you focus your attention on this it will simply create unwanted tension. Take a step back and do something that the horse understands well. If you keep trying and this does not work, you can try to put your weight on the inner buttock bone. Some horses react well to this because it motivates them to move on to their inner front leg and place it under the rider when picking up pace. You can also try to keep riding lightly; many horses find it difficult to accept the movement of a rider that keeps sitting on its back. You can also try to ride lightly on the inner front leg or taking in a contrasting position (letting the horse look to the outside). However, the horse does not learn much when an insecure rider tries one thing after the other. A good instructor can help you here; not only with picking up pace, but with the rest of the training of the horse.

Never forget to reward the horse

11. Frequent rider mistakes

Instructions
A good instructor can help in preventing the following mistakes and can also correct them. Just about every mistake is caused by the rider. Good horse riding lessons can prevent errors from creeping in. Someone who is judging from the ground how communication between the horse and the rider is going can often form a good impression of the ability of the rider.

Pulling in the bend
Unfortunately, many riders make the mistake of wanting to let the horse walk by pulling at the reins. This is not nice for the horse; and in the long run not good for the rider either. A horse that has problems with the rider's hands will never look to be leaning back but will be hiding with its head behind the lead line to have as little burden from the bit as possible. In common terms this is called "pulling in the bend." This may seem nice to a novice, but an expert will immediately see that the horse is not walking fluently with its body and that the hard work from the back part has disappeared. The leaning has disappeared because the horse is trying to pull back from the rein commands. There is no

Behind the lead line

Against the reins

contact with the rider's hand; the horse does not want to feel the bit because it is irritating it.

A pulled- away back like a plank

Against the reins

It is also possible for a horse to react to the hard hand of the rider by "walking against the reins." Instead of hiding behind the lead line, the horse is bringing its head far beyond the lead line and is thus creating counterpressure to the rider's hand. The horse is pushing its back away so that you cannot ride it anymore. A good rider feels the back usage of his/her horse immediately when the horse is not being used in the correct way; a relaxed back sits like an armchair and a pulled-away back like a plank. Only a soft hand can ride a young horse with the reins. A horse that stubbornly refuses to bend its head down must have bodily complaints: back problems or hurting teeth, for instance. It is very important for a horse dentist to have a regular look at the teeth of a young horse.

Striving too quickly to erectness

Only at a later stage of the training, when the horse is walking relaxed with the back and bends itself forward-downwards, can we work towards erectness and collection.

- **Erectness**

Being erect is where the horse slightly changes its head and neck posture, which will make it walk slightly more upright. The highest point of the horse will become the point between the ears of the horse.

The young horse will not be sufficiently developed to collect and walk upright after 1 to 2 years of training

• Collect

In order to collect, the hind legs must be placed even more under the body mass, with the horse placing its weight a little more to the back. The weight of the rider, which is placed on the front part of the horse initially, is to be carried by the back legs. This will lead the front part to become more erect while the back part will fall away a bit under the extra weight.

The horse will in fact be "sitting." However, at this stage of the training this is not yet under discussion. A young horse is walking wide with its back part and to collect the horse will have to make a narrower set of tracks with its hind legs (the hind legs must be closer to each other). The back side must be able to drive first of all, in order to be able to carry the weight and this requires further training. Only after 1 to 2 years of training will a horse be developed sufficiently to be able to work on collecting and walking erect. Even if this may not seem nice, there is nothing that can be done about it yet: first of all forwards-downwards, then erect. First drive, then carry.

The horse falls over the front side

It is literally hanging with its mouth on the bit

Falling towards the front

Some riders are so occupied in making their horses lean forward-downwards that that the end-result is a horse that is falling towards the front. The back part is in this way physically coming off from the ground with the horse walking with its nose on the ground. You can basically say that the horse is "walking on its head." The horse will in this way be hanging on its bit, which the rider will realize when his hands and arms become tired from carrying the weight. This is not the aim. If a horse is falling too much to the front, you can correct it by driving the horse forward and picking up the front part a little more. Some horses react well to the rider suddenly letting go of the mouth while driving forward so that the horse will literally be biting the dust. It is often a question of experimenting to see how the horse will react to a specific method.

Not for the leg

Many riders have the tendency to not support a horse with a natural liking for running with sufficient supporting calf commands. This is due to an – unfounded – fear that the horse will start to run too quickly. The horse is not activated enough by the legs because the rider is pushing his/her calves down and they do not stay in contact with the body of the horse. In this way the horse will always react badly worse to the driving calf commands. This can be prevented by explaining driving commands to a horse with a natural forward tendency by using a whip to assist if the horse does not react immediately. The bottom part of the leg must stay next to the horse because it is necessary to "keep the horse in its place" when turning.

The horse is not making proper tracks

"Not tracking" means that when a horse is walking along a long turn, it is not well aimed. The back legs do not run in the same line as the tracks of the front legs. This often happens when the horse is not well in balance. In the beginning you should practice many straight lines and not constantly ride in the open. In this way the horse will learn how to aim well and keep walking well under the legs of the rider. At a given moment the horse will have to learn how to react to a one-sided calf command when you start using the calves to indicate away movement. You can practice now already how to direct well on a long direction line and using one-sided calf commands. The horse must learn to react to the command by placing its back part in line with the front part so that all four legs can carry an equal distribution of the weight. If the horse does not make good tracks during a turn it will be because it does not bend well length-wise. It is bent too much or too little whereby the hind leg is not right walking right behind the front leg.

Well aligned; this horse makes a good set of tracks

Not aligned correctly

The horse is not standing squarely

"Standing squarely" means that the horse is standing with its front legs and hind legs respectively directly next to each other when it is standing still. At the beginning of the training, it is too early to strive towards this. Only a horse that is walking with good balance will stand squarely. Once a horse is used to walking in balance, it will place itself squarely when coming to a halt. Take note: a rider must give the command at the right moment when the horse comes back, and must give the horse the calf command to keep it from standing still immediately. A horse that is prepared through a semi-delay will be ready to halt and will have learnt through weight assistance how to "come back" or reduce the tempo and will stand squarely. Do not try to correct the situation after halting. Steps to the front and steps to the back do not work; halting correctly must sprout from the working tempo.

Dressage trial

In order to ride dressage trial, it is of course essential for the horse to understand and obey rider commands. The idea is for rider commands to be given to the horse more and more subtly with the passage of time. This means that you must feel the horse even better and it must react to the slightest change of weight or the smallest calf command. In order to reach this, the rider must be clear and consistent and know that it is very important that the horse must keep liking the

After such an extended trot you should not push too hard with a young horse

Even if the horse is tense, it should still listen to you

work. Do not practice the entire dressage too frequently with the horse, but rather perfect the sloppy parts. The trial run will be frequently changed and most horses can forget a trial run as quickly as you can. It is a boring ride if the horse knows everything almost before you do, but practice the change and turns well:

• Change
The horse must be able to walk the change in a relaxed way without its head coming out in front of or behind the lead line. Perfect the change and prepare the horse with a semi-delay before the change. Teach it to increase the pace and then to bring it back down again when you request it to come down. Do not get angry when the horse goes over to a gallop when you only wanted it to trot. You should always look at yourself first of all when there are mistakes. In the lower dressage classes, all changes can be made progressively. You have enough time to prepare for the change over in a neat way, so use the time.

• Turning
Riding through many turns will make the horse supple and teach it to bend around your inner leg. Even though "turning from the calf" is not required in the first dressage trial, it is handy to teach the horse now already how to react to one-sided calf pressure. Practice this to the full, for instance by increasing the openness or decreasing it through calf commands. Teach the horse to always go through the turn with the correct posture and prevent it from falling back from its tempo. Support the outer front side of the horse during the turn with your outer hand and prevent it from swinging out its back side by keeping your outer leg against the horse.

Tip
Before you bring it out for the first time, take the horse to the competition terrain so that it can get used to the hectic activities there.

*Riding outside
offers a change
for the horse*

Ensure variation

It is important that your horse keeps enjoying itself. For
this reason you should vary the work by letting it trot over
rails. Start with a single cavaletti over which the horse must
calmly walk (be careful: some horses take a giant leap the
first time). After this you can start expanding it. Lay the
cavaletti a distance of three feet away and calmly trot over
it. Try to make the horse walk forward-downwards, always
in the middle of the rails. Walking over cavalettis encoura-
ges the suppleness of the horse, and most horses like doing
it. Jumping over a low obstacle is also a good way to put a
young horse to work. Start with a cross that must be jum-
ped over with a trot at the end of a row of cavalettis. In the
beginning the free standing obstacle must always be approached with a trot and a ground rail must be placed about a
foot away in front of the obstacle. Only once the horse gallops calmly away after the jump (and this can sometimes
take up to a few weeks or months) can the cross be approached at a gallop.

To the outside

Riding outside can be a welcome change for both the rider and the horse to relax after dressage work. It is also a good way to make the horse used to all different types of circumstances. Only do this once the horse can gallop and once you are sure that you have the horse under control. If you are going into traffic, it is a good idea to take an experienced horse with you the first time. A young inexperienced horse will learn in this way that it does not need to fear traffic or anything else that it may encounter outside of the usual riding area. The combination of an anxious horse and busy traffic can be very dangerous, not only for yourself but also for the other road users. Riding outside is great fun for most horses (and their riders), but only those horses that have been trained well!

12. ACKNOWLEDGEMENTS

Acknowledgements

The author and publishers wish to thank the Drurens stable in Druren, Ton van Bragt, Janneke Verschure, Rene Otten and the Haaglanden police for permission to photograph them.

Literature used

Longeing with Lammert Haanstra, Lammert Haanstra
The Horse Whisperer, Monty Roberts
The Ease of Dressage, Claartje van Andel